This Notebook Belongs To

© 2020 Eunoia Journals

PISCES - THE TVELFTH ASTROLOGICAL SIGN

Pisces are very friendly, so they often find themselves in a company of very different people. Pisces are selfless, they are always willing to help others, without hoping to get anything back.

Pisces is a Water sign and as such this zodiac sign is characterized by empathy and expressed emotional capacity.

Their ruling planet is Neptune, so Pisces are more intuitive than others and have an artistic talent. Neptune is connected to music, so Pisces reveal music preferences in the earliest stages of life. They are generous, compassionate and extremely faithful and caring.

People born under the Pisces sign have an intuitive understanding of the life cycle and thus achieve the best emotional relationship with other beings.

Pisces born are known by their wisdom, but under the influence of Uranus, Pisces sometimes can take the role of a martyr, in order to catch the attention. Pisces are never judgmental and always forgiving. They are also known to be most tolerant of all the zodiac signs.

Element: Water
Color: Mauve, Lilac, Purple, Violet, Sea Green
Day: Thursday
Ruler: Neptune, Jupiter
Lucky Numbers: 3, 9, 12, 15, 18, 24

Want information about spirituality and self-improvement?

Visit www.eunoiajournals.com

There you'll find a special gift that will allow you to go on a life changing journey as well as more information about how YOU can cultivate mindfulness, productivity and happiness.

Follow Us On Social Media:

Instagram @eunoia_journals

Made in the USA
Las Vegas, NV
21 April 2024

88964046R00069